DATE DUE

MY 1 08			

DEMCO 38-296

Moon Go Away, I Don't Love You No More

The Miami University Press Poetry Series
General Editor: James Reiss

The Bridge of Sighs, Steve Orlen

People Live, They Have Lives, Hugh Seidman

This Perfect Life, Kate Knapp Johnson

The Dirt, Nance Van Winckel

Moon Go Away, I Don't Love You No More, Jim Simmerman

Moon Go Away,
I Don't Love You No More

Poems
by
Jim Simmerman

Miami University Press
Oxford, Ohio

Copyright © 1994 by Jim Simmerman
All rights reserved.

Library of Congress Cataloging-in-Publication Data

Simmerman, Jim, 1952–
Moon go away, I don't love you no more : poems / by Jim Simmerman.
  p. cm. — (Miami University Press poetry series)
ISBN 1-881163-09-1 (pbk.) : $9.95

PS3569.I4726M66 1994
811'.54—dc20   94-14637
                                                                CIP

The paper in this book meets the guidelines
for permanence and durability of the Committee
on Production Guidelines for Book Longevity
of the Council on Library Resources. ∞

Printed in the U.S.A.

9 8 7 6 5 4 3 2 1

Maureen

*as if to say elsewise
would make it unso*

Acknowledgments

The Antioch Review: "Vesperal" (Copyright © 1992 by The Antioch Review, Inc. First appeared in *The Antioch Review*, Vol. 50, No. 4, Fall 1992. Reprinted by permission of the Editors.)

The Chariton Review: "Maddy's Woods"

CutBank: "Bumblebee" and "Fly"

Denver Quarterly: "Take What You Want but Eat What You Take"

The Journal: "Beast Zoo," "Inside Out," "Money," and "Outside In"

The Laurel Review: "Hide Away" and "Wheel"

The Nebraska Review: "Blind"

Negative Capability: "Bushhog" and "Dim"

New Letters: "Cheers" and "Yoyo" (First appeared in *New Letters*, Winter/Spring 1990, Vol. 56, Nos. 2/3. Reprinted with the permission of New Letters and the Curators of the University of Missouri-Kansas City.)

Northern Arizona Review: "Omnipotence"

Off-Season, The Provincetown Fine Arts Work Center Anthology: "Love Skull"

Ploughshares: "The Public Job of Blood" (First appeared in *Ploughshares*, Vol. 13, No. 4, December 1987.)

Poetry: "Distance," "The Glass Park," "Kite," "Just to Love the Dog," "Moon Go Away, I Don't Love You No More," and "Take a Hike"

Sonora Review: "Bluebird in the Rain" and "Take It Back"

Southern Poetry Review: "Night of the Living Dead"

Tendril: "Grievous Angels" (First appeared in *Tendril* Magazine under the title "The Reluctant Angels.")

Writers Forum: "Tell Them"

Some of these poems were earlier collected in a chapbook, *Yoyo*, published by GreenTower Press.

The author is grateful to Northern Arizona University for organized research support which helped make possible the writing of this book.

Contents

1

Take It Back	3
Fly	5
Bushhog	6
Blind	10
Dim	12
Maddy's Woods	14
The Glass Park	17
Distance	20
Cheers	22
Take What You Want but Eat What You Take	24

2

Omnipotence	31
Moon Go Away, I Don't Love You No More	32
Vesperal	34
Tell Them	35
Grievous Angels	37
Money	39
Love Skull	41
Night of the Living Dead	42
Bluebird in the Rain	44
Take a Hike	47

3

Wheel	51
Inside Out	52
Outside In	54
Yoyo	56
Kite	60
Beast Zoo	61
Bumblebee	63
Just to Love the Dog	64
The Public Job of Blood	66
Hide Away	67

1

Take It Back

Maybe it's different
with you. How I grew up
there was always some kid
bigger than me, some lug,
some stupe, some Ronnie Boone
with fuzz over his lip
and those muscles you get
squeezing tennis balls,
skulking on the playground
before homeroom or glued
behind some tree somewhere
I have to pass alone
and—boom—he's on my chest
like a stump, slapping me
daffy, his knees gouging
gopher holes in my arms
as he croons *take it back*,
so soft and close and sweet
he could be telling me
a secret or kissing me
on the mouth, *take it back
if you know what's good for you.*

Some things I did I didn't
take back. I could

say one, embarrass us
all for a time. Then you
could take your turn, then
somebody else, until
the bullies inside us
get bored and go home;
till we're each of us smack
on his back by himself
in the same stupid life,
and we do it again—
the whole thing pathetic
as a push-and-go-round
where I stick to my guns,
and stew, and spin—the same
tune repeating itself,
the same verse, the opus
of Ronnie Boone: *take it
back, take it back if
you know what's good for you.*
Which I don't though I do.

Fly

I wish I could sing like hummingbirds fly.
I wish I could hear the flowers.
One day the leaves on the aspen are green.
One day you tremble for hours.

One day you feel like a cross without tenure.
One day, like a kid with a match.
I wish I could just blow away like the clouds
or snuff all the stars with a breath.

I wish I could take back the last wish I wished.
But I can't, and I can't wish it harder.
One day the world doesn't matter so much.
One day it's meaner and smaller.

One day they dress you in clothes of glass.
One day they board up your eyes.
I wish it wasn't so far to fall,
wasn't so hard to fly.

I wish I could go where hummingbirds go
when flowers thud deaf on the lawn.
One day the leaves are waving goodbye.
One day the leaves are gone.

Bushhog

Winter is eating the country again,
devouring alike the quick and the dead.
At five I'm awake and dressed of habit,
and feed myself to the ineffable
machinery of its weather, the gears
of ice whirring and grinding in place.
A raw wind chews its way through the body,
gnaws at the nerves and licks the bones lean.
The industry of winter is hunger:
its teeth at the throat of everything.

All one winter my job was to clean
gearbox housings at the Bushhog plant.
For hours like years I sloshed those hollow
steel skulls in a drum of gasoline
until the skin peeled from my hands like bark
and my head was a blizzard of fumes.
In the worst weather in decades, regardless
whether I had slept or not, I rose
each morning before dawn, dressed in stiff jeans,
and drove myself back to work again.

That early, the houses I passed looked dead.
And I felt like a ghost, like nothing
could see or touch me. I felt like all
the stiffs who drudged in silence beside me
at the factory—building a machine
that could bite its way through brush and timber—
must have felt every day of their dead lives.
Lost in the body's mechanical plod
and the mind's bad weather, we reentered
together that shadowy world of machines

that could chew a finger clean off a hand
before the nerves could run it to the brain.
Everyone there was mangled or scarred.
In safety glasses and steel-toed shoes
we filed past the time clock, feeding it
the bent, oily cards that wore our names.
A few dingy lightbulbs flickered overhead
like listless stars on a cloudy night.
Steel dust snowed into our nostrils and mouths.
Everyone there was being eaten alive.

That was the winter my warm-blooded dreams
died of exposure. That was the winter
I huddled inside a thin coat of sweat
and let myself expire from the heart out.
Each night I lay in bed shivering,
praying to the god of absolute zero
for some sleep. Each day I grew less visible,
answering to *You* or *Numbnuts* or *Boy*
for a few worn dollars and pocket change,
understanding I understood nothing

beyond the din of presses and lathes
banging senselessly against themselves,
beyond the assembly of drive trains
hanging like carcasses from grappling hooks
and the relentless business of making it
from one day to the next without screwing up
or wearing out or breaking down, feeling
nothing beyond the cold and the ache
and the dead heft of the gearbox housings
that weighed on my hands like time itself. . . .

I thought then nothing could kill me again,
but mornings like this I see I was wrong.
I see how the world eats your heart out
day after day after day, like a bushhog
chewing up everything in its path,
ripping it apart and grinding it down. . . .
The next time I pray let me fall to my knees
at the mouth of whatever needs to be fed
the blood and the bone and the flesh of it all.
The next time I die let me stay dead.

BLIND

You can stare at my face
as long as you want to.
All up and down my body
you can run your eyes.
It doesn't matter.
I won't even notice.
It's true I'm blind
and therefore not entirely human—
in some ways more like a fog
with legs,
in some ways more like a vine
that noses and knocks its way
to where it needs to get.
It's true you're kind
to offer to guide me
to an empty seat
where you can watch my fingers
do their little twitchy dance
and study the absolute
zeros of my eyes,
maybe get a good look
inside my blouse or up my skirt
and wonder what it's like
to fuck a blind girl.
I don't mind.

I don't have to see you
to know the blunt
instrument you've made of sight,
or to know your world
with its glitter and glare
is still a cave
you're lost inside.
I can smell the animal
of you like a fever.
I can hear every click
of your brain like dice.
What do you think?
What does it matter?
You've never seen nothing
every day of your life.

Dim

Mostly I chart the hour by the minute.
Mostly I navigate time.
Anymore a good day is where I don't capsize in public,
don't spill things too often,
manage to keep the car between the lines.

It's cold. It's winter—why wouldn't it be?
Mostly I can't sleep right,
but sit up pretending I still know how to read
or watch TV—the words look foreign;
the mouths and voices don't synchronize—
or eyeball the plants, how little they change,
so I can't tell whether they're growing
or dying or what, anyway, they're supposed to mean,
or how anything bides the night.

There's a streetlamp burning dim outside.
Its job is to prove no one's there.
Its job is to prove how dark and peaceful
the rest of the houses in the neighborhood are,
like ships at rest in a calm harbor,
like tomorrow they could be going somewhere.

Oh, I know there are stars and planets to steer by.
I know how things can change overnight.
But it's cold and it's dark and a long drift to morning,
not marooned from the heat so much as the light.

Maddy's Woods

That crusty, good man John Fife
pretended to blow his nose. . . .
In just one night her breathing

had grown labored, raspy
as a punctured squeeze-box;
her mouth cold, a pocket of ice.

I pretended, earlier, in the dark
back room, to follow the concise
lesson in black and white

textbook photos, in shadowy
x-rays, back-lit, pinned to the wall
like the pelts of ghosts:

how the normal canine heart
is ovoid, a fist-sized egg
in the nest of the ribs;

and how this one's heart
had enlarged, swelled up
like an over-inflated balloon. . . .

By now she could hardly walk.
By now she was wrapped
in a blanket on the floor,

and when she raised her head
once, to look around the room,
her eyes saw what?—

we might have been mist;
we might have been aspens
rooted in snow. It's time

to go walking in Maddy's woods,
where a hawk throws a shadow
you could chase through the trees,

where the tough, thorny branch
of a wild rose clings
to a little scrap of fur,

and all those smells
on the breath of the wind
make you crazy in the nose.

It's time to go
down on all fours and dig
deep into the frozen bed of the woods,

and let the heart rest
that ran so hard, that grew
too big for this world.

The Glass Park

There's a glass bird in a glass tree
and you have to like the fountain
shimmering beneath a glass sun
so brightly you could cut yourself

just staring at its beveled spray.
The children, who are also glass
on their glass slide and their glass swings,
could make you cry big glassy tears

for how they look like figurines
gathering dust on a bookshelf
in a room where a real child lived
once. There's the tune the glass bird sings

and each note is a little globe
of translucency as it floats
out on the cut glass breeze of May
or April, which also carries

the scent of rain. There is the same
glass man reading the same glass book
and he can look right through each page
to the end. There is the woman

underneath the glass parasol
and above her, a single cloud-
like pane; and the light's falling down
and around and through all of it,

magnifying and refracting
as inside an aquarium.
There's the glass boat with its glass sail
etching a pond that's also glass,

and the glass swans glisten and break
from its surface like a mobile
hung from an invisible strand.
Also, there are the two glass dogs,

their glass tails wagging as they sniff
after each other's genitals.
There are the glass flowers nodding
over their glass stems and the bees

are harmless and ornamental.
Likewise the heart is made of glass
and doesn't so much beat as thrum.
And the glass blood in the glass veins

is a fragile laboratory.
And the transparent horizon
is a window you can see through
from one thing into another:

into the glass face in the glass
face looking back at and into
and through you with its eyes like cheap
interchangeable glass buttons.

There is the glass earth like a glass
tray, and the sky is bottle blue.
There is the one glass rock the size
of your fist. You know what to do.

Distance

Everyone knows what the shortest distance
between two points is. And everyone knows how
there's an infinite number of points in between.

Imagine applying Zeno's Paradox to the phone company:
none of your calls would ever get through, but then
you wouldn't get billed for them either.

It's like trying to decide whether the glass
is half-empty or half-full when you'd just
as soon throw it back and pour another.

But the point is, sometimes you *have* to decide—
like pitching to the clean-up hitter:
Slider? Curve ball? Power against power?

And when the ball thumps off the bat—it's timing—
a good outfielder can tell *just by the sound*
which way to run, and how far, and how fast.

And the fans shoot straight up out of their seats
without thinking how knees are supposed to work,
and their shouts converge like a connect-the-dots puzzle.

Imagine yourself driving back from the game—
you're a little exhilarated and a little bored
and there's nothing, really, waiting at home

so you decide to meander, your car a duck
doing a cursive duck-glide down a road
that shimmers in the heat like a river.

Maybe the road runs next to a river.
You park, take off your shoes and socks,
roll up your pants and wade on out,

just standing there while the sky goes dark—
just standing there till you really can't say
where your body ends and the water begins;

or how the day got so quickly away;
or when the first grain of starlight appeared;
or whether your life's half-empty,

half-over, half-hearted, or just poorly timed.
Imagine yourself trying to come to the point
from such distance and so out of line.

Cheers

Because lonesome is a party
of uninvited guests, because
each guest is the self
and the self won't behave,
but drinks too much and
talks too loud and grinds
his cigarettes out in
the carpet, embarrassing
everyone finally with his
petty revelations and his
boozy promenade, because
everyone loves a party
but no one wants to clean
up after, and because
you can measure how good
the party was by how
much mess was made and
by how little everyone
remembers later—some
of them so shitfaced
they had to sleep over—
and because some things
are best forgotten anyway,

and basically because you
can't remember having
ever been so lonesome
in your life, though
basically you were most
every day, but thought
the company not so bad—
sweethearts really, if
a bit morose—the conversation
basically okay, the liquor
loose, the music soft,
the occasional slow-dance
alone, you raise your glass
like a flag of surrender
and—*Cheers!*—the party's on.

Take What You Want
but Eat What You Take

I can't recall whether my assignment
is to say what it's like or what it means.
Either way, I know that the alignment
gets squirrelly by and by, and know that streams

flow in only one direction. Memory
gets to be like a telescope that chooses
for itself which end fits up against the eye,
blackens it sometimes (some joke!) when I use it

to spy too hard or too long on something
that's better off forgotten. For instance,
the time I told a lie that went running
tattle-tale off on its own like some fitness

freak, some Paul Revere of mendacity,
and left me cramped and huffing way behind.
There are other lucid transparencies
to lay atop that one—you know the kind—

like in the anatomical textbook
I'd hunker over in the library,
just a kiddy trying to sneak a peek
at a titty or a snatch. It was scary

how I had to work my way through the bones
and muscles, the liver and intestines:
all those parts I've lately come to know
stall out, wear down, call for the question

again and again long after the quorum's
been lost. Clearly, the body will break
your heart like kindling. Meantime, a forum
of another sort fires up, and one side takes

the position that the difference between
love and *in love* is the same as that
between *correct* and *incorrect;* and it seems
like someone, some dewy-eyed Webster type,

would compile a dictionary of
the affections, where whatever gets felt
gets alphabetized where I could look it up,
gets spelled out and defined, even gets dealt

into a pithy, illustrative phrase
I could enunciate, though the rhyme
and reason escape me. At my age—
which is the line people use to remind

me I'm somewhere in the middle of things—
things I ought to know still catch me by surprise
(pants down, day-old underwear gaping
at the crotch) like houseguests who arise

before I'm awake enough to recollect
they're there. It's like the mind plays hooky.
Sometimes my own words are weird and suspect
as something out of a fortune cookie.

It's from a Chinese smorgasbord place
in San Diego I get my motto:
take what you want but eat what you take.
It's true! They charge for the ginseng jello

uneaten on your plate, fifteen cents,
two bits for barbecue chicken feet.
(I couldn't afford my own bad taste, hence
ended up ditching them under the seat.)

What else have I ditched? (O rapid turn
in this stream of talk I didn't mean to take
so loosely rigged!) It makes the brainpan churn
like a voodoo cauldron of eyes and snakes

to think of things I might or might not have
done, things I can no longer do or undo
and—no—I won't be supping with the saved.
I've had sufficient. May I be excused

from the moderate mess I've made of my plate
if I promise to brush my teeth and floss
and gargle away the aftertaste?
Give my compliments, please, to the chef.

Although I didn't save room for dessert,
I'll palm it into my pocket, then home—
another sweetness I'll break to read: *regret,*
regret and plenty more where that came from.

2

OMNIPOTENCE

A stylized tomfoolery. A bit
in the mouth of a dream. Omnipotence
has its limits, as any deity
could tell you (if the phone would ever ring).
Meantime the world's an interminable
tease: box inside a box inside a box. . . .
You'd as well torch the maple in May
of its leaves as ransack the snow for a rose.
You'd as well face a mirror and cajole
yourself daft ("After you, Cap'n Hubris,
after you. . ."). *Noah Don't Surf* is
one play for which I'm still waiting on
the reviews. Imagine it this way:
we each get a turn (the house lights darken;
the rest of the principals clam up
and fade). In God's wading shoes I know what
I'd do and it wouldn't take forty days.

Moon Go Away,
I Don't Love You No More

Morning comes on like a wink in the dark.
It's me it's winking at.
Mock light lolls in the boughs of the pines.
Dead air numbs my hands.
A bluejay jabbers like nobody's business.
Woodsmoke comes spelunking my nostrils
and tastes like burned toast where it rests on my tongue.
Morning tastes the way a rock felt
kissing me on the eye:
a kiss thrown by Randy Shellhorse
on the Jacksonville, Arkansas, Little League field
because we were that bored in 1965.
We weren't *that* bored in 1965.
Dogs ran amuck in the yards of the poor,
and music spilled out of every window
though none of us could dance.
None of us could do the Frug, the Dirty Dog
because we were small and wore small hats.
Moon go away, I don't love you no more
was the only song we knew by heart.
The dull crayons of sex and meanness
scribbled all over our thoughts.
We were about as happy as headstones.
We fell through the sidewalk

and changed color at night.
Little Darry was there to scuff through it all,
so that today, tomorrow, the day after that
he will walk backward among the orphaned trees
and toy rocks that lead him
nowhere I could ever track,
till he's so far away, so lost
I'll have to forget him to know where he's gone.
Le poulet grave du soir est toujours avec moi—
even as the sky opens for business,
even as shadows kick off their shoes,
even as this torrent of clean morning light
comes flooding down and over it all.

Vesperal

Moonlight. Rune light. Blank
to blanker pages of wind-expunged dunes.
Soon it will be required of you to speak of this;
soon to say, in a language lost or uninvented,

what it is comes stealing through the dark
to darker June night, post-equinox,
ghost-key to locks on doors like mute,
bewildered faces. Think of yourself as an oasis.

Think of the vast, unquenchable caravan of souls.
Perhaps there are holes through which the dead slip
back into being. Perhaps, even now,
they are preening in the seethe and hiss of a dervish sky.

Hush. Listen. Do you hear your father calling
and calling you to supper? Do you want to go?
No. Nor is the moon a communion plate.
Nor are the stars drops of spattered wine.

Not this time. Though the thought of it flares
like a candle touched to the brittle parchment of night,
you do not kneel down, nor look away;
and you hold your tongue, for now, spoon-tight.

Tell Them

Tell them I was last seen a heart-lope away
from the bridge between Holyoke and Chicopee, Mass.,
in the goose-pimple sun-up of April or March
in the year of the fire trap and the year of the match.

Tell them I was wearing a plaid snap-brim cap
and a thin windbreaker with a broken zipper,
that my face was polished an industrial gray,
and I looked like arson, and I smelled like sulphur.

Tell them I had no identifying marks
beyond the kind of ears that snuff out speech,
and the kind of gapped teeth you can spit through,
and eyes the color of old meat.

Tell them my hands were raw and split
and brushed my legs through the holes in my pockets.
Tell them my trousers were long and frayed
where they dragged between my shoes and the concrete.

Tell them my shoes were leather or canvas.
Tell them my hair was crew cut or long.
Tell them the sun rose red from the river
like the fiery face of a delinquent god.

Tell them I was wired, or strung out, or reckless.
Tell them I was broke, or breaking apart.
Tell them the wind felt the way the phone sounds
when you keep on listening after someone's hung up.

Tell them I was proud or ashamed of myself.
Tell them the river was dirty and cold,
and that the sirens came moaning on all at once,
and that I signed my name in illegible smoke.

Tell them I would have done anything then
for anyone else who had bothered to care.
Tell them I'm gone like the last chance they had.
Tell them I was there.

Grievous Angels

New York City is one place you find them,
huddled in stairwells, frayed sweaters crammed
with yesterday's news. Hope, Arizona,

another, meandering its lone street
long after dark, sifting the desert
through tattered boots. Or threading

the backroads through some failed town
or another, you'll spot one frozen
in a thicket of weeds—a scarecrow

left standing one too many seasons,
a monosyllable of stunted speech.
In Coos Bay, in interminable rain,

you'll see them sweeping at flooded gutters.
In Starkville or Carthage or Union Square,
remanded to benches in public parks

and muttering to anything there
won't mind: mongrel, statue, swing set, whatever. . . .
They are like ghosts with permission to haunt

themselves feckless. They are like gods
in which no one any longer believes.
They are like the indelible crosses

on the windows of condemned tenements.
Like a train wreck they go on and on—
in Muleshoe, in Man, in Zion, in Clay,

in the ward no one visits, in shambles,
in the ice-fringed shawl of winter, inane,
in the paupers' graves of their own shadows. . . .

They are always lost; they are always alone
and hugging themselves like distraught lovers.
They're the grievous angels of hell on earth:

their wings are ablaze; their wings won't open.

Money

This morning the sun comes up all copper,
though I see it first reflected in
a neighbor's window—as if the sun
were rising inside a house! And maybe
it's true there's a kind of dawning going on
in each of these homes I pass this morning—
myself a sleepy citizen bent
on the ordinary chore of commerce
as I trudge through cold December weather
to the convenience mart for a paper
and a pack of cigarettes—for each house
I pass has a window, and each window
has a sun, and each sun is like a coin
of fire blazing, there, where I can see it
for so long as I can hold my gaze
against such opulence. I have the bills
and change to pay for what I'm after,
though I'll pick a penny or two from
the dixie cup beside the register
to make the deal precise, and exchange
small chat about the economy
with the man behind the counter. And later,
maybe tonight, when the sun has set
and the town is dark and cold and half-asleep,
I'll give a cigarette to someone who

asks for it, plus another, for later,
for when he's alone and the spark and warmth
of an ember will be some company.
There are, I know, those cultures where a bone
or a bead will purchase something dear.
And those others, mostly dead or undreamed of,
where symbol is so sanded that need
is currency enough. But I live here,
in the wallet of America, where
what passes for money passes from hand
to hand like a baton in a relay race
where the runners keep stumbling over
the junk accumulating in their lanes.
Though for now it's the sun, the real sun,
that has risen high enough to squander
its heat and light on anyone who cares
to open a door and step outside
on a fairly common, cloudless day
when it can dawn on you to assess
the worth of a coin by watching it shine,
by hearing it chime when you toss it away.

LOVE SKULL

sits in the middle of Lovers' Lane
like a speed bump in a morgue;

has a grin like a hook and a wink like bait;
has a shark finning round in its heart;

has a tattoo that reads "Love Skull + _____ ,"
then below that, "this space to let";

has a word to the wise you don't get to hear;
doesn't forgive; doesn't forget;

doesn't do poems, ponies, or proms;
keeps a Valentine's scab in a jar;

has a kiss that can stand on its hind legs and bark;
drools like a festering sore;

hoodoos your brain like a mine on a mission;
coos in your ear like a thorn;

thinks you're a sweetie-pie, cute as a button
gnawed off the blouse on a corpse.

NIGHT OF THE LIVING DEAD

Fortunately the dead move slowly.
They're dead. They're all messed up.
The bad news is: they've got us outflanked,
outnumbered, bamboozled and on the run.

Beat 'em. Burn 'em. They go up
pretty easy. But sure as *shazam*
there's a passel more—groping
the grille-work outside the window,

incorrigible salesmen with their feet
in the door. Their dead white feet
and what they're selling's no life-
time enrollment in dance academy,

no new-fangled gizmo for tucking
the tummy, no minty elixir
for the heebie-jeebies.
Fair is fair. The dead are dead.

But mainly they're just like us:
doomed to redundancy, pushy
and scared, unlucky at cards,
unlucky in love. Mainly

the dead are the living in drag—
that's one way to figure the gossamer
garb, the pancake make-up
that streaks down their cheeks.

No wonder they stick to the dark.
No wonder the dead have so little
to say, no wonder they travel
in packs. No wonder they look

on the living as meat, a raw
ratio of protein to fat.
It's what keeps the living
dead on *their* feet, dead

tired, dead drunk in the dead
of the night. It's stuck
as we get on our own quickened pulse.
It scares us half to life.

Bluebird in the Rain

So far as I know
there was nothing in it
for him. He just sat there
on the house-for-sale sign

while rain slugged down
around him and around
the face of the fogged-up
car I was dry inside.

So far as I know
he had no business there
unless there is business
in public sogginess

and passing for what looked
to be a small blue flame.
On a slick mountain road
where driving means business

I was headed hard home
and not given over
to happy distraction.
Anyway it was cold

and rainy and though still
only late September
I had a mind to break
old boards into a nest

from which to nudge the soft
blue feathers of a fire.
Otherwise why was it
I was worrying so

the gas I all but failed
to notice how he sang
a song so A-B-C
another man might have

braked right off, two-stepped out
into the rain and perched,
singing along for nothing
but the harmony?

How do I know what
another man might do?
How do I know the song
was happy? All I know

is a fire no bigger
than a bluebird kept
someone warm and singing
lo a cold night. Plenty.

Take a Hike

I don't mind taking a hike in the woods.
There are stones like ellipses for crossing the creek.
I can abide the stuffy silence of owls

that spy from the branches without spectacles,
and like how their heads work. Plus, there are leaves
that are more like the rough drafts of leaves

and remind me the world is working
things through by gab and revision—like you,
like me—and knows when to edit, and knows

how to use, without showing off, its big
vocabulary. So what I can't name
the bush with thorns like fire on my cheek?

My flesh has the language for what happens next
and runs-on the sentence without skewing
the meaning and the blood's red penciling

is part of the text. The rest of the story
is a matter of stump rot, weather, hills,
and a lot of loose talk. How, anyway,

can you tell a flower from a weed
if both are comely? I'm beholden
to the author and the publisher, both.

3

Wheel

Don't fall in love before you've made the wheel
your study. See how it crushes and churns
unsullied on to the next disaster.
See how it burns like the hoop an animal
learns to leap through for its supper. Study
the heart and its demolition derby.
Study the shadow that merry-go-rounds
the sundial. Meanwhile, there are things like rings
that slip from the hand and roll under places
you'll never look beneath. Things like a wreath
of riddance, like a halo for the blind
pedestrian reading the street with a cane. . . .
Study the wheel stripped of steering and brakes,
the wheel you'll have to reinvent again.

Inside Out

Because you leave mysterious droppings in the burners
    on the stove.
Because their smoke intrigues me when I brew coffee.
Because your car drips oil all over the garage.
Because I only see it when you're not with me.
Because your hair, your hair's all over the house.
Because I pick it up. Because it thrills me.
Because you sleep so late the rubber tree is dying.
Because the bed's an insomniac without you.
Because I do the dishes and I make the sandwiches.
Because I don't even like bologna.
Because you ask me to dinner means I pay.
Because alone is lousy with anchovies.
Because your car's real name is Vanna, the Color of Itself.
Because *your* real name is Olga Stubendougall.
Because you're secretly a black girl disguised as a white
    girl.
Because you're a peanut disguised as a woman.
Because I begged two months for your paisley shirt.
Because you wouldn't give it, no way.
Because I sulked in private and you never knew.
Because when I wear it in San Diego it'll drive the girls
    crazy.
Because you make my knees sing Motown.
Because you taught my lips to dance.

Because my heart was a drummer all these years and
    never even knew it.
Because wanting you is the emotional equivalent of
    drinking from a dribble glass.
Because I can't fire you and you won't quit.
Because I'm so scared you'll leave me I drive you away.
Because I'd sooner your fibs than God's own truth.
Because if I'd written this sooner maybe you'd have stayed.
Because this ain't no poem, it's my love song to you.
Because World Beyond is I'm Sorry.
Because love is a racehorse named Clementine.
Because given its head—oh—my darlin'!

Outside In

It's like getting a card that reads:
sorry to hear you cut your finger
off with a knife. Signed,
the knife.

It's like body-surfing in broken glass.

It's like taking a called third strike—
two down, bases loaded—in the ninth inning
of the seventh game of the World Series
of the rest of your life.

It's like trying to talk a cadaver into smiling.

It's like sewing with a needleless thread.

It's like spelunking a cave that gets smaller
and darker the farther you get into it—

only you *are* the cave, it's like that.

Or like performing open-heart surgery in mittens.

Or like washing your face in gas.

Or like eating the Gobi a grain at a time,
then the Mojave, then the Sahara. . . .

It's like the algebra of infinity raised to its own power.

It's like falling in love where *love* means *space*,
keeping your dark side to yourself
like a moon.

It's like reading a long, sad novel
where in the end they shoot the racehorse,
then you have to bury it with a spoon.

Yoyo

I can only think I've killed something.
Years back, when I was a kid and not
supposed to know anything more or less,
just visiting some distant country
cousins down round Piggott and St. Francis,
Arkansas, I *wanted* to learn hunting,
wanted to rise *with the birds* is what
they said—oh, I remember liking that,
like we'd all just open our eyes and stretch
our arms and fly right out the windows,
maybe circling the farmhouse once,
maybe thinking one last time how strange
to be a naked boy a hundred foot
above the dark woods and bottomlands;
then, only the wind and the light-
boned dip of wings beating the earth back
a flap at a time, only the sun
spinning up like a yoyo in the east.

Yoyo, they said, like *Chrissake* or *Goddamn*,
Yoyo—meaning me. Doves were in season
and any farmboy could have told you
how simple it was to squat in the bed
of a slow-rolling pickup truck and pick
the little feathered buggers off the limbs

of maple or magnolia trees, pop them
from the powerlines where they perched in pairs
and threes like smalltown gossips gathered
after church, drop them even where they drifted
gingerly as love notes posted on the breeze.
So what to make of a crazy kid cousin
ripping along ahead of the Ford—
shoelaces flopping, shirttail unfurled—
flailing his arms like wings almost, almost
a bird himself as he screamed *fly away!*
fly away! for all he was worth? Yoyo.
Doves. St. Francis. That's not what I mean.

I can only think I've killed something.
Now that I'm a man and not supposed to
act the fool anymore, but walk on
two legs and be of one mind and keep
the heart hidden away like a housebird
caged and covered for the night; now that
I've fallen in love for all I'm worth—
fallen like a shot dove plumb-lining to earth,
fallen like a yoyo that can't climb
its way back to the hand; now that all I'm worth
is a handful of words so petty
and polite I could dangle them from a string,

attempt a trick or two perhaps, perhaps
get one thing finally right for you
to see, and shake your head about, and walk
as surely away from; *now* I get it,
finally, like a shot upside the head:
Yoyo, you killed it. Yoyo, it's dead.

Once I was four on *The Fred and Fay Show*,
the birthday boy on local TV.
I was made to be king and to wear
a paper crown. I was made to stand up
as they said my name wrong. I was made
to applaud the Yoyo Man as he spun
his way through a dozen foolish tricks:
Lunar Loops (the orbit a tangle)
and Around the World (he snapped the string).
To finish, the Yoyo Man spilled from a sack
a cheap plastic yoyo for each child there.
Somehow it figures: he couldn't even count.
The yoyos ran out with the kid to my left.
I cried and probably crapped-up the show,
but after—listen, here's what I mean—
the man took the hand-carved mahogany job
he told me he'd had since *he* was a boy
and slipped it onto my finger like a ring.

Maybe he lied and maybe he didn't.
The thing is, always, there's something left
to give so long as you give a damn at all;
one dove drifting over the feckless fields,
always, no matter that you lost the farm;
no matter that I lost the yoyo
years ago and never missed it till today,
or the Yoyo Man and all he was worth—
Rock the Baby, Walk the Dog—who must be dead
by now with "Yoyo Man" carved above his grave.
I can only think I've killed something.
But still I act like it's alive, like
it'll come dragging itself home somehow and
so I suppose my cousins were right:
I'm a yoyo. I'm a yoyo man
with a yoyo heart and a yoyo brain,
duping myself with a dozen dumb tricks,
everything flying out of my hands.

Kite

Here's what I get for being a cross on a sail.
Here's how I jitterbug light.
I don't say it's dull, but mainly
I'm pretty uneasy up here—exposed and nervous.

Mainly I'd rather not fly
in one place with my tail traipsing down
like a dog that's been beaten,
like a cow shooing gnats.

Mainly I study the ground
just looking for someplace to land
without smashing myself to smithereens;
or stare off into the distance—

which is farther up here, and
clearer, and more empty than you'd suspect—
like a prophet without a vision,
like a corpse with a few regrets.

I'm tied to a string. It runs from the fist
of someone probably knotted-up as me.
I don't say whose fault it is. I'm a kite—
I don't say anything—

waiting to be reeled in or cut free.

Beast Zoo

The words willy down like cod liver oil,
like cod-liver-oil-soaked peanuts.
The kind of peanuts you feed to the beasts
at the Beast Zoo in Merkel, Texas.
Texas, whose state flower is the dung rose,
whose state bird is the cankered dove.
Texas, smelling of singed fur and fever
and sprawling out beyond the windshield
like all the dead letters that sign off *with love*.
What are we doing there, 1979,
in our bruise-blue Buick with the windows
rolled up—temperature 112°—our hair
wadded into Beast Zoo caps, the doors locked?
What are we thinking that we don't think
to hear the hiss from the hole in the radiator?
And that's what it is. And that's how we steer
like a shot moose to the side of the road
with the radio coughing *la cucaracha*.
And that's how we come to the Beast Zoo Motel
with its grocery sack walls and its talking toilet.
On toward evening, down by the pool
where Kleenex and gum wrappers soak up chlorine,
there's this lady decked out in a wedding dress
and sneakers, walking a monkey on a leash.
"It's a working monkey," she explains in slow-motion,
like we're slow children. "It ain't got no teeth."

And the monkey grins and scratches its crotch,
and the plastic palm trees nod in agreement.
It's our honeymoon is what you need to know.
We think we're in love and that we know what it means.
We think we can keep loping on and on
like the unfenced miles of empty plains
squinting up at the sky going black in the east
like a patch of skin at the end of infection.
We think we're inoculated, clean.
Then this: someone says something mean
and unmeant, though the second part hardly matters
once it comes clear how the chain of events
is a durable leash tugging hard at the collar.
Later that night, logged into bed
like the effigies kids build to fool their parents,
we're eating our words a course at a time,
we're choking them down letter by letter
like bad little monkeys made to clean their plates—
but all this in silence, in a Beast Zoo Motel
where the wages of whimsy are peanuts to gum
and the check is always in the mail.

Bumblebee

The fattest one I've seen this month
of Sundays; so close I see it's woolly,

a little head with wings. How it got
here—stuck between the bedroom window

and screen—I can't imagine. No cracks or tears
so far as either one of us can see.

I'd let it out if somehow I could figure
the trick it takes to unattach the screen;

but letting it out means letting it in
and though I spot no stinger, still, I'm cautious,

no fool for harm. I'm no soldier, no sir,
but know it's tougher living in the gap:

the glass so clear you can't not see what's past it,
the mesh so fine the pollen drives you mad. . . .

If the rabbit dies we won't have the baby.
"Don't want it," she says, like "it" was a name.

My daughter or son, my no-one-to-be,
how I wish we could all bumble free as we came.

Just to Love the Dog

Just to love the clock again.
Just to love the chair
that rocks a little

when you rock a little
sitting in the living room
you're living in

alone again.
Just to love your share
of channels that stay up all night:

the Dream Away plan, the news
that hasn't changed
since yesterday,

the late late show
in which the dead arise
and walk and die again,

the forecast high in Gila Bend.
Just to love the telephone
for how it hunkers down

and doesn't ring
or dial or hope or fret
about itself. Just

to love the dog again:
the tongue that licks
the hand, the paw

that shakes, the ears
that prick like someone's
coming back.

The Public Job of Blood

What we wondered as kids about the light
in the icebox we're wondering now
about love. The apple digesting itself
in the pantry. The corpse in need

of a shave. All that goes on when no one's
around to see it or say what it means.
All the king's horses dead on their feet,
the fastidious glue of dreams. Last night,

tucked away in our separate beds, did we
fall out of love into sleep? Did the stars
boil down to a soupy incandescence?
Did the moon rot away like rancid meat?

Romance is a perishable gourmet
gyp, like those dyed flakes of fish face
fobbed-off as crab. If the public job of blood
is to bleed, its private job is to scab.

Hide Away

You can't know what the future holds,
she tells me. Like the future is a pair of hands—
a lover's, say—balled up and held
in front of me and I'm supposed to pick between
the one that's empty and the one that's full
of nothing I can begin to imagine,
and whatever's there, that's what I get.

From morning into afternoon we've traced
the narrow switchbacks that connect
county to county, mountain to desert, winter
to spring to get to where we are:
the Hide Away Lounge, and we try, watching
tourists watching tourists, reciting lines
about where we're going and what went wrong.

I tell her most of what I know about the future
is what I know about the past, how—no—I can't *know*,
but can guess—how everything connects
anymore in the heart's crazy wiring,
how everything plugs into something else
the way the VCR plugs into the TV set so you can
tape a movie one day and watch it another.

I tell her how the day before I watched
Love Among the Ruins, how Katharine Hepburn
and Laurence Olivier—"she ruined my life,"
he says, and *means* it—fall back into each
other's lives after almost fifty years.
So maybe she's right, maybe people *do*
hook up again, I say. In movies.

I tell her how in the movie's climactic scene
Olivier quotes Browning—"Grow old along
with me"—and how I knew the line from
a John Lennon song. I tell her how it was recorded
in one take on a home cassette machine,
John singing it to Yoko, accompanying
himself on piano and beatbox;

and how I hadn't known it was Browning,
and how the song was never meant to be released;
how all of this is *after* she kicked him out,
after eighteen months' separation
during which she stayed in New York City
with their son Sean while he stayed, with Ringo
and Harry Nilsson, drunk in Los Angeles.

Everything connects. I tell her how, *before*
the movie, I got a call from my ex-wife,
how we hadn't spoken for seven years, how
passion can go haywire, can grow so hot
you have to jam a tool into the works,
and how that tool, that torque-wrench silence,
had cast a shadow over me since.

By now afternoon is running into evening,
the tourists are touring somewhere else.
Shadows are sprawled all over the place,
but I can't stop talking or thinking
or feeling, can't stop tracing the wires
that run off every which-way, that knot
and tangle and loop back over themselves.

By now I can't *not* tell her how, between
my wife and me, there had been a few weeks
we were so broken down we thought we could
build ourselves back from scratch, collect
the junk and patch it together some new
or different way to make the whole thing
run again without burning out the circuitry;

how all this happened at the same time
John and Yoko got back together to make
Double Fantasy, how hopefulness
loves its symbols, and how the single
from the album had just been released:
"Starting Over" pouring out of every radio
and jukebox and tape deck in the city.

I tell her how I can't, finally, hide away
from any of this, because everything connects
like those Christmas tree lights where
when a bulb blows they all go out
and you have to test them individually,
work your way along the whole string—
how one thing fails and it all shuts down:

how because another woman I loved let my dog
out one morning, how because the dog was
hit by a car, and because that dog
replaced somehow another dog I'd lost—
a dog that was all of what I had
left to keep alive and care for
of my marriage—the woman and I broke off;

how it took years to figure this out;
how Hepburn says to Olivier, "I too
have cherished hopeless hopes," meaning
nothing by it since she still doesn't
remember him, and how most of the film
is a blueprint of missed connections since
Olivier's doom is to remember everything.

I tell her how I remember everything
about the day Lennon was shot, how friends
I hadn't heard from for years called—
the phone lines everywhere so tied up
you'd have thought it was Christmas—
how an ice storm buried the whole Midwest,
how my wife and I buried the last of our vows.

I tell her how I buried the first dog
in a blizzard, wrapped in a blanket
from my marriage bed. I tell her how,
with the other woman, I buried the second dog—
the last loving thing we did together.
I tell her how I don't know how to even
begin to bury this thing between us

because neither of us knows how not
to love the other any longer though
neither of us knows how to do it right,
and because *it*, by now, is so
hashed over and reflexive and familiar
it's like we're watching ourselves in a movie
we've watched often enough to know by heart.

I tell her how each night my dreams
are so much like my life I can't tell
anymore if I'm awake or asleep.
I tell her how each day is so much
like the day before I can't imagine a future
any different from this, how everything
connects and connects and connects

and I don't know how to make it stop,
don't know how to unravel the wires
or work the controls to turn it off.
"Consider the boy who loved you," quotes
Olivier, "believing that you loved him. . . ."
Then the movie ends and the tape
rewinds and it all starts over again.

Jim Simmerman is the author of two previous books of poetry, *HOME* (selected by Raymond Carver for a Pushcart "Writer's Choice" citation) and *ONCE OUT OF NATURE* (chosen for the Best of the Small Presses book exhibit at the Frankfurt Book Fair). His poems have appeared in a variety of journals and anthologies, including *ANTAEUS, IOWA REVIEW,* and *POETRY, THE BEST OF INTRO, THE BREAD LOAF ANTHOLOGY OF CONTEMPORARY AMERICAN POETRY,* and *WESTERN WIND.* The recipient of fellowships from the National Endowment for the Arts, the Arizona Commission on the Arts, and the Provincetown Fine Arts Work Center, he is Professor of English at Northern Arizona University in Flagstaff, Arizona.